# INTERNATIONAL POLITICS

DR. BANTI KUMAR

Made with ♥ on the Notion Press Platform
www.notionpress.com

# Contents

# Acknowledgements

Acknowledgement

Firstly we would like to thanks Chound Mata, the tribal goddess of Gaddi Tribe for blessing us with a great work. We are also thankful to Prof. B. L. Sah, Ex. Director UGC-HRDC Kumaun University Nainital Uttrakhand for helping us in our research studies. We are also thankful to our parents and other family members for their moral as well as financial support. We are also thankful to our teachers Master Kans Kumar and Sh. Sishpal (Accounts Officer) for guiding us. We are also thankful to Principal Sir, all our colleagues from Govt. Degree PG College Bhaderwah and Library Staff for making available some good books in library. We are also grateful to Prof. Neeta Bohra HOD, Prof. Madhurendra Kumar, Prof. Kalpna Agrari and Dr. Hirdesh Kumar from Department of Political Science, Kumaun University Nainital Uttarakhand for their valuable teaching methods. We are also thankful to our friends including Dr. Pawan, Dr. Bhumika, Dr. Anita, Dr. Kailash and Dr. Sumit for their friends company. Last but not least I am very thankful to our parents and other family members for moral as well as financial support especially our son Advik and Devansh for their valuable smile.

CHAPTER ONE

# Meaning and Approaches

**International Politics, meaning, Changing Nature and Scope:**

**International Politics:** The word '***International Politics***' is a combination of two English words i.e. International and Politics. The word 'International' was first of all used by Jeremy Bentham in 1780 when he talked about 'International Jurisprudence'. He used it to for the branch of law which commonly goes under the name of law of Nations. Since then this term is used to relation between different nations. The term Politics is derived from Greek word '***Politikas***' which means concerning the ***city states*** or *the* ***citizens.*** In simple language it is a branch of Political Science or International Relations which deals with political relations between the two or more countries. Various thinkers such as Hans J Morgenthau and Kenneth Thompson have used International Politics and International Relations synonymously. International Relation is a broad field which covers the political as well as non-political relations between the two countries. International Politics is a part of International Relations which covers the political relations between two countries. It is related with the Government, Political Parties, Power, shift in power and political offices. It mostly covers the official relations between two countries. It is simply the Politics in relationship between nations.

**Definitions:**

International Politics is the relations among the states **Charles Schleicher**

International Politics is a struggle for power among nations **Hans Morgenthau**

International Politics covers those aspects of interactions and relations of independent political communities in which some elements of opposition, resistance or conflict of purpose or interest is present **Harold and Margaret Sprout**

International Politics is the interaction of state policies within the changing pattern of power relations **Norman Vadelford and George A Lincoln**

International Politics refers to a process by which conflicts arise and are resolved at international level **Charles Reynold**

**Evolution of International Politics**

As a subject matter, it was also present in Greek period during time of Plato and Aristotle. It was also present in India during the time of Kautilya. Out of the 15 books of Kautilya one was for diplomacy. Machiavelli's 'The Prince' was also about the suggestions for king about his policies for survival and expansion of State.

In 1919 ***Woodrow Wilson Chair*** was established in University of Wales (UK). Prof. ***Alfred Zimmern, Sir Charles Webster*** and ***E. H. Carr*** all historian were the early holders of this chair. 1920 International Relation (IR) started its journey as independent subject in American Universities. In USSR International Relation was treated as branch of History even after World War $2^{nd}$. It was treated as a part of history in Moscow State University even in 1960s.

**Stages of Evolution**

a. **First Stage:** This stage runs up to the First World War. International politics was taught by diplomats, historians who were interested in history than in politics. Their main concern was the description of past events rather than the analysis of present and their projection for future.
b. **Second Stage:** This stage starts from the end of First World War and in it only the study of current affairs was stressed. Hence

like first stage, this approach was also partial.

c. **Third Stage:** It also began after the First World War and continued to exist throughout inter-war years and even after. Suffered by the First World War, the prevailing thinkers tried to give emphasis on the reformist view. Much hope was raised by the League of Nations which was expected to replace narrow nationalism to internationalism.
d. **Fourth Stage:** It came after the Second World War. The War and its devastation showed people's faith in the utility of international organizations and law as instrument of peace. The emphasis shifted to making a scientific analysis of the developments in international politics.
e. **Fifth stage:** This stage lasted from mid sixties to the seventies. In this stage the post realist paradigm is appropriately labelled the behavioural approach to the study of international politics.
f. **Sixth stages:** This stage runs from late seventies to the first half of eighties. During this period doubts were raised on the efficiency of the detente and the new detente emerged. Soviet Union intervened in Afghanistan and US threatened the world by talking of Star War programme.
g. **Seventh stage:** This stage began in 1985 when Mikhail Gorbachev came on the scene. International relations have passed into a quantitative new era with the advent of Gorbachev's new political thinking for the world.He applied the policy of Peristroika and Glasnost in the Russia which finally lead to disintegration of USSR.
h. **Eighth stage:** This stage commenced in the early nineties when discipline of International Relations witnessed another turning point with the disintegration of Soviet Union as a super power. Republics of the USSR and Yugoslavia became independent states. On the other hand European states emerged as united in the shape of European Union.
a. **Ninth stage:** This stage started with the coming of 21st century. In the first half of this century the doors of the international politics were opened by the globalization. The role of various

agencies such as World Trade Organization (WTO), Multinational Organizations (MNCs) and Non-Governmental Organizations (NGOs) become important in the international politics

**Nature of International Politics**

International Politics is of following nature

a. Sovereign States are its chief Actors
b. International Politics is struggle for power
c. Protection of National Interest is the Objective
d. Conflicts are condition of international Politics
e. Power is both a means as well as an end in international Politics
f. International Politics is a process of conflict resolution among Nations.
g. International politics as a system of continuous interactions among Nations.
h. International Politics has its base in Behavioural Study
a. Inter-disciplinary Study is also its integral part.

**Changing Nature of International Politics:** During the ancient time International Politics was a subject matter of making war alliance or doing a peace treaty. Due to the limited means of communication it was limited to a limited area. With the improvement in means of communication its nature also changed from war and peace to various other situations.

First big boost in the development of its nature came with the treaty of Westphalia in 1648. This treaty gave the concept of national state in International Politics. It recognized the nature of national self determination. National state is the only point from which the societies can interact with each other. After it the official relations between these national states improved the character of International Politics.

From a small area under its influence changed to a large area with the development of this subject. Before the First World War it was limited to a region of the world but after War period its influential area increased to include the whole world. After the war period the League of Nations played an important role in improving the nature of International Politics.

The incident of Second World War developed this field more with open diplomacy between different countries and the influence of democracy. We cannot forget the contribution of United Nations in changing the nature of International Politics by motivating the member countries to improve the official relations among them.

With the passage of time International Politics too kept crawling. Its nature got a big boost with Liberalisation, Privatization and Globalisation. The Multinational Companies working on the world level, Pressure Group and Non-Governmental Organisations forced the national government to improve the international politics. World level problems such as terrorism, environment degradation and recent the COVID-19 pandemic also contributed in changing and improving the nature of International Politics.

**Scope of International Politics:**

The scope of International Politics is not yet well settled. It is continuously expending. H. Morgenthau holds that struggle for power among Nations forms the scope of international Politics whereas Burton holds that besides other things, the study of International Relations includes all conditions and factors which influence the behaviour of more than one state. These views highlight the diversity that prevails among scholars regarding the scope of International Politics. Followings are the some of the scope of International Politics.

a. **Study of State Systems:** Its base of study is the State System. It studies state so that it could suggest best measure to improve it.
b. **Study of relations among states:** It also studies the relationship between various states. By improving the mutual understanding of the two countries, it avoids the war like situation.
c. **Study of national Interests:** It also studies the national interest of a country and how it changes with time. It suggests best

measures to modify national interest so that country could develop peacefully.

d. **Study of national Power:** It also studies that national power. It is an important factor in power politics.
e. **Study of foreign policy:** It is an important aspect of development in modern times. International Politics is so deeply concerned with it that sometimes International Politics is also called Foreign policy.
f. **Study of international Law:** It also studies the international law as of UNO and International Court of Justice.
g. **Study of International organizations and institutions:** It studies various international organizations as well as institutions. SEATO, UNO, SAARC, BRICS and ASEAN etc. are its examples.
h. **Study of war and Peace:** Study of war and peace are its two important aspects. The study of one is important for other.
a. **Study of Conflict Management and Conflict Resolution:** It studies various methods to avoid conflict and make a resolution of any dispute between nations.
j. **Study of Ideologies:** It studies the various ideologies of world such as liberalism, communism, capitalism, Marxism and socialism etc.
k. **Study of Nationalism, colonialism and imperialism:** It also studies the nationalism, colonialism and imperialism.
ax. **Study of Disarmament:** It focuses much more on the study of disarmament. Various disarmament packs between USSR and USA during cold war are its best examples.
all. **Study of the issues related to environment Protection:** It studies the environment related problems and try to solve it on national and international stages.
n. **Study of the issue related to Human Rights:** It studies the human right problems in various parts of the world. Various NGOs are financing research work related to Human Rights in International Politics.

**Study of the role of Economic Factors:** It studies role of various economic factors. The factors responsible for the poverty among the developing as well as developed countries.

**Idealist Approach in International Politics or Idealism in International Politics**

Idealism emerged in 18th century and is regarded as a major source of inspiration behind American Revolution (1775 – 1783) (American independence in 1979) and French Revolution (1789 -1799). In International politics it remained as a dominant philosophy between the two World War Periods. According to idealist thinkers the society and state are outcome of evolution. This process of evolution is leading this society toward perfection from imperfection. At this stage peace and justice can be established in the society. Through the establishment of a family of nations, war, violence and immorality can be curbed. Condorcet, Woodrow Wilson, Butterfield and Bertrand Russell are some of the Idealist thinkers.

Basic Assumptions: Following are some of the assumptions of the idealist thinkers

a. **Human Nature:** They believe in the good nature of human being. They are capable of altruism, mutual aid and collaboration.
b. **Fundamental Motive:** The main motive of human being is welfare of other and made progress possible in the society.
c. **Evil Institutions:** Bad human behaviour is not due to their own nature but because of some evil institutions which promote them.
d. **War:** It is the worst feature of International System.
e. **Elimination of War:** War is not inevitable and can be eliminated by doing away with the institutions that encourage it. E.g. Military Industrial Complex (John Kennedy US President was supposed to be killed by MIC)
f. **Problem of War:** War is not a national problem. It is an international problem, so it can be sought out by international

efforts.

g. **International Society:** This has recognized itself for elimination of institutions that make war likely.

**Suggestions for reforms**

a. **Moral Principles:** All the nations should behave morally by elimination old practices of capturing power.
b. **International Institutions:** To replace the current system of territorial state. They demanded the world federation or one government.
c. **Legal Control:** They demand for new trans-national norms to check institutions of war. E.g. Kellogg-Briand Pack 1929.
d. **Elimination Weapons:** Eliminations of weapons is the basic need for avoiding any future war and achieving peace. E.g. Washington Naval Conference 1920s.
e. **Elimination of Totalitarian Forces:** Elimination of Totalitarian Forces from this world is necessary to achieve the peace in this world. Totalitarian forces in the history have resulted in war. E.g. Hitler in Germany and Mussolini in Italy.
f. **Restructuring international monetary system:** International monetary system should be restructured to eliminate the trade barriers in international trade. Some writers have suggested the self determination of nation.

Woodrow Wilson is known as father of idealist approach (Idealism) in international politics. He has given his ideas in his famous fourteen points in his address to US Congress in which he stressed need of USA to enter the world war in order to make the world safe for democracy. These 14 points are mentioned below;

i. Open diplomacy without secret treaties.
ii. Economic free trade on the seas during war and peace
iii. Equal trade conditions
iv. Decrease armaments among all nations

v. Adjust colonial claims
vi. Evacuation of all central powers from Russia and allow it to defend its own independence.
vii. Belgium to be evacuated and restored.
viii. Return of Alsace-Larraine region and all French territories
ix. Readjust Italian borders
x. Austria-Hungary to be provided on opportunity for self determination
xi. Redraw the borders region creating Roumania, Serbia and Montenegro
xii. Creation of a Turkish state with guarantee free trade in the Dardanelles
xiii. Creation of an independent Polish state
xiv. Creation of the League of Nations

**Criticism**

The idealist thinkers were criticised by realist thinkers for their idealistic thoughts. International relations changes with time and every nation tries to increase their power. So there is no relevance of idea in international politics. Hans J. Morgenthau, E. H. Carr, Kenneth J. Thompson, Reinhold Niebuhr and George Kennan were the main thinkers in criticism list.

**Realist Approach in International Politics or Realism in International Politics**

Realism developed in the post Second World War period in reaction to an older theoretical approach called 'Idealism'. Idealism emphasizes on international law, morality and international organization as key influences on international events besides power. Idealist believes that human nature is basically good and the principles of international relations must flow from the principles of good morality. Human being has the capacity to work together to solve common problems. The idealist approach was dominant between the First and Second War period. Woodrow Wilson and other Idealist so called the ***'children of light'*** had hope from the League of Nations. After the outbreak of Wold War Second this philosophy was criticized by Realist thinkers.

Realism is also known as '***Political Realism***' or '***Realpolitik***'. The tents of realism place national interest as the most important priority of a state. This does come at a price, which is often violence as the two world wars have demonstrated. If each state is committed to a path of power aggrandisement wars are frequent occurrence. The principle line of thinking of the realist is in terms of power and its exercise by states. It is based on '***realpolitik***'. The word '***Realpolitik***' was coined by German philosopher ***Ludwig Von Rochau.***

**Historical background of Realism:**

Thucydides an ancient Greek historian wrote ***'History of Peloponnesian War'***. He is also known as father of Realism. Chanakya wrote ***Arthashastra***, Machiavelli wrote '***The Prince***', Hobbes wrote The ***'Leviathan'*** and Carl Von Clausewitz wrote '***On War'***. All these writing were related to realism.

Realism remained as the dominant political philosophy throughout the World war 2nd and Cold War period.

**Assumptions of Realism:**

a. **Anarchy:** There is anarchy in international system i.e. complete lawlessness in this world. It is based on the principle of might is right. Nations has to depend upon themselves for their own security.
b. **Principle Actors:** States are the principle actors in the international politics. If there will be any conflict in international politics it will be between states and if there be any peace talk it will be between states.
c. **National Interest:** Every state has its national interest and there is difference between their individual interests. (Opposite to harmony of interest as claimed by idealists.)
d. **National Power:** Every sovereign state tries to increase their power by means of national interest. They pay a heavy price for achieving this power in the shape of war with human loss.

e. **Relations based on Power:** The relations between states are based on the power of the state. A powerful state is treated as superior in International politics as compared to less power states.
f. **Actions of the State:** National Interest guides the actions of the state. Every state acts according to their own national interest.

Chief exponents of realism are E. H. Carr, N. J. Spykman, Reinhold Neibuhr, George F. Kennan, H. J. Morgenthau, Kenneth W Thompson and they are commonly known as children of darkness. E. H. Carr criticised the idealist in his famous work '***Twenty Year Crises 1919 – 1939***'. Realism is the first school of thought in International Politics.

It is often said that realism is international political theory is nothing but realism and other school of thought are nothing but only footnote to realism. Realist thinkers are also known as children of darkness.

E H Carr did not explain the theory of realism he only did a critical analysis of the idealism and undermines it influences. The credit of giving full explanation of Realism goes to Hans J Morgenthau. He was a Jew who reached the USA as a refugee having faced racism in Germany. Due to his persona; experience he was strongly against the totalitarianism and weak foreign policy to deal with such tendencies as reflected by idealist in International relations. Hans J. Morgenthau in his work '***Politics Among The Nations: the Struggle for Power and Peace***' gave 6 principles as given below

a. **Objective law of human nature:** Politics is governed by objective laws based on human nature. Politics is shaped by human nature. Hence the scientific understanding of human nature is the basis of formulating the scientific theory of International Politics.
b. **Interest in terms of power:** Every state tries to acquire power through their national interest. He views the international

politics as a process in which national interests are resolved on the basis of diplomacy of war. Power acts as the end as well as the means of national interest.

c. **National Interest is dynamic:** National interest is not fixed it remains changing with environment and time. There are no permanent friends as well as enemies. So there are no fixed national interests once for all. It changes with situation, time and financial condition. Minimum national interest is the survival and maximum depends upon the time, condition and situation of country.
d. **Universal moral principles:** They cannot be applied to state actions. They must be filtered through circumstances of time and place. Every state behaves immorally to acquire power for security. There is no room for ethics in the international relation. Every country works on the principle of separation between ethics and politics to maintain their identity.
e. **Moral aspiration of a nation:** Political realism refuses to identify the moral aspiration of a particular nation with moral law that governs the universe.
f. **Autonomy of Political Sphere:** The Political realism maintains the autonomy of the political sphere. Politics is not economics as Marx thinks, it is not law as jurist thinks and it is not ethics as idealist thinks. It is autonomous and has its own laws

Hans J. Morgenthau is also known as father of realism in International Politics or simply father of political realism. During the post-cold war period realism faced much criticism. Kenneth Waltz updated the realism to suit it in the post-cold war period. This updated version of realism is known as neo-realism and the realism before this period is known as classical realism.

It is believed that realism is still a dominant philosophy. This point can be verified that within a short period of huge damage of humanity and resources with COVIS-19 pandemic, Russia and Ukraine are involved in a long time war. This situation is so bad that instead of doing a ceasefire and peace treaty the UN permanent members are fuelling the war by supplying weapons to the Ukraine and imposing economic sanctions on Russia.

**Criticism:** Realist approach dominated the world after the World War Second and also during the Cold War period with Soviet Union intervened in Afghanistan and US threatened the world by talking of Star War programme. The situation changed with the coming of Mikhail Gorbachev came on the scene in 1985. He applied the policy of Perestroika and Glasnost in the Russia which finally lead to disintegration of USSR simultaneously the end of Cold War. After the end of Cold War realism philosophy was too criticised and a new modified version of realism came to scene known as neo-realism or contemporary realism.

## Neo-realism

Realism was criticised after the 1990s by a group of thinkers particularly known as pluralist thinkers. Realist believed that state is the only actor in international relations. This view of realist was challenged by the pluralist. Pluralists emphasised the fact that state may be the significant actor in international relations but it is not the sole actor. They acknowledge a plurality of actors in international relations such as MNCs, NGOs, other organisations and the nature of people as well as system of Government. This pluralist challenge was soon met by a new brand of realism in the writings of Kenneth Waltz which is known as neo-realism or contemporary realism.

Kenneth Waltz in his famous works ***Man, the State and War*** 1959 & '***Theory of International Politics***' 1979 came up with his idea of world politics which is known as ***neo-realism***. In these books he was influenced by microeconomics. He addressed the defects of realism in his writings. Morgenthau used the normative approach in his concept of realism. E. H Carr modified realism under the light of science and reasoning. Behavioural movement also played an important part in influencing the neo-realist thinkers. Neo-Realism is also known as ***structural realism or contemporary realism***. Kenneth Waltz argues that self interest motivates a state to protect its security. In this anarchical world the absence of an overarching authority above them, states are forced to restore to self help.

He argued that in this international system there is anarchy. In this anarchic condition, in order to survive there is only one option that is self help. For this self help, states try to increase their power (weapons etc.). This process leads to a severe '*security dilemma*'. Security Dilemma means security builds of one state leads to the insecurity of other and hence other state will also react to build their security. He differs from classical realist thinkers on two issues. First, the source of conflict or cause of war do not lie in human nature but within the framework of anarchy where states have no recourse but to go for self help to protect themselves. Second, in this environment of anarchy a *balance of power* will occur which is like more *balance of capabilities* instead the *balance of power*.

According to Kenneth Waltz there are two factors which impede the cooperation in this anarchical international system i.e. insecurity and relative gain. It was relative gain that both USA and USSR instead of ideological differences came together against Germany during world war second.

Within the sphere of neo-realism some other standards have emerged as discussed below

a. **Defensive realism:** Kenneth Waltz, Van Evera and Jack Synder argue that states are not intrinsically aggressive or militaristic. Since the costs of war generally outweigh its gains, nations have no reason to be overly militaristic. War among great powers occurs largely because of misplaced perception of threat and overzealous conception of war. In simple words they believe that military setup and increasing the defence power is for self defence purpose.
b. **OffensiveRealism**: Randall Schweller, Eric Labs, John Mearsheimer, Fareed Zakaria and other offensive realist believe security competition and dilemmas will never disappear entirely from world politics and the basic parameters of the international system will remain the same i.e. anarchical. For this reason all

states would try to maximise their relative power in global politics. It was supported by John Mearsheimer in his work '***The Tragedy of Great Power Politics***' (2001). He argues that states are power maxi misers. In short they believe that state acquire power for offensive purpose.

Reinhold Niebuhr has tried to bring idealism and realism together. In his writings '***The Children of light and the Children of Darkness 1944***' opines that it is possible to combine the wisdom of the realist with optimism of the idealism. One can also discard pessimism of the realists and foolishness of idealist. In short unlike the realist according to neo-realist national acquire power not as an end but as a means. They acquire the power as a means for their ultimate end i.e. national security which is very important for the survival of a country. It also relies on the principle of microeconomics. It claims to be systematic and scientific as compared to classical realism. Neo-realism was also influenced by behavioural 1960s.

**Criticism**

a. It stresses solely on power and power struggle i.e. power monism.
b. It puts great emphasis on power politics, state sovereignty, balance of power and war without much focus on peace process.
c. It makes negative assumptions about human being such as rational pursuit of self interest, utility maximization which are hardly verifiable.
d. Benno Wasserman, Robert Tucker, Stanley Hoffman and others criticise it on the ground that it is neither realistic nor consistent with itself.
e. Quincy Wright criticised it for totally ignoring impact of moral values on National policy.
f. Tickner criticised it by blaming it as a partial description of international politics by ignoring the woman in their approach.

CHAPTER TWO

# Key Concepts: National Power and National Interest

**National Power: Meaning, Forms and Role**

Power is simply defined as the ability to dominate the other person. Hans J. Morgenthau defined the power as "***man's control over the minds and actions of other men***". Thus the political power is the relationship between the holders of the public authority and the people at large. According to Hans J. Morgenthau, political power is a psychological relation between those who exercise it and those over whom it is exercised. Power possessed by a national is called national power. Power in the international relations generally denotes the ability of one nation to force the other nations to do the favourable things, which would other-wise not have done. Capturing of oil fields in Iraq by USA, threatening neighbouring countries via its border disputes by China, applying economic sanctions by USA on Iran and North Korea, defending Bhutan against Chinese aggressive policy and Balakot Strike of India on Pakistan etc. are some of the examples of National Power.

Following are some of the definitions of power in International relation

**Hartmann:** 'Power lurks in the background of all relations between sovereign states'.

**Kautilya:** Power is the '***possession of strength***' and is derived from three elements i.e. Knowledge, military and valour.

**Robert Dahl** "ability to shift the probability of outcomes"

**Padelford and Lincoln** "National power is the sum total of the strength and capabilities of State".

**Hartmann** "The strength or capacity that a sovereign state can use to achieve its national Interest"

**Anam Jaitly:** "a capacity to influence people domestically and other nations externally towards certain desired national preferences".

**Ebenstein:** National power is more than the sum total of population, raw material and quantitative factors.

**Organski** "Ability to influence the behaviour of others in according with one's own ends".

**Forms of National Interest:** There are mainly three types of power i.e. Physical, psychological and economic powers as described in brief below

a. **Physical power:** Military strength of a country is known as physical strength. USA, Russia, China, India are some of the physically powerful countries of the world. Government of a state enjoys the physical power because of the subordination of military power to political power. Whenever this subordination is disturbed it results in snatching away of political power as seen in Pakistan after 1999 Kargil war and same case seen in Myanmar in 2021.
b. **Psychological power:** This power was enjoyed by the nation and is based on public opinion. This power is mostly identified by propaganda. This form of power was responsible beyond the successfulness of Fascism in Italy under Benito Mussolini and Nazism under Hitler in Germany. China is also using its power to threatening its neighbouring countries in border disputes.
c. **Economic power:** This power is also very important for a nation for its survival and growth. This form of power is also linked by military power. If a nation will achieve its national interest it will

become powerful and military capabilities will held it to fulfil these interest. During this current time USA is supposed to be more powerful as compared to Russia due to economic strength of former.

**Methods of exercising power:** Following are some of the methods to exercise power.

a. **Persuasion:** In this method a nation persuades the other for favourable decisions. This method diverts the mind of other nation. This method is followed in most of the international organisation by its member countries. This method is used by strong states for weak states. It was used by China & USA against various small countries.
b. **Reward:** This method was also used by strong economic country against a weak country. In this method the strong country offers financial or material aid to the other country for taking it in their favour. Providing financial aid to Pakistan by USA for her establishing a military base during war on terror in Afghanistan. Moreover the USA and Saudi Arabia's relations including stability of govt. in Saudi and marketing of oil in dollar are also linked with reward.
c. **Punishment:** Reward and punishment are closely linked. If the country still not assures the favourable decision by taking reward, the strong country threats for punishment. Applying economic sanctions on Iran and North Korea by USA are its best examples.
d. **Forces:** A threat of punishment is a preventive measure but if it too fails for taking a weak state in favour, it takes the shape of force. Force is supposed to be very destructive as it may lead to a world war as seen in history.
e. **Skill:** It plays an important part in exercise of power. It includes the taking right decision on right time, avoiding anger etc. e.g. a wrong decision of declaring a war can lead the countries in the darkness.

**Conclusion:** It can be concluded from the above discussion that power is an important element in international relations. Every country is known by the power it have. Increase in Powers of one nation leads to decreases in power of other nation. It can be of Physical power, psychological power and economic power. It can be applied through persuasion, reward, punishment and force depending upon the nature of native people as well as system of government.

**Elements of National Power: Tangible and Intangible**

National power of a state depends upon various factors. These factors are called as elements of national power. Different thinkers have given different categories of elements of national power. Hans Joachim Morgenthau has divided them into two categories i.e. permanent and changeable.

Abramo Fimo Kenneth Organski classified them into natural and social determinants. The natural determinants are geographical, natural resources and population. The social determinants are economic development, political structure and national morale. Edward Hallett Carr gave three categories i.e. military power, economic power and power over opinion. Palmer and Perkins divided them into tangible and intangible. Tangible elements are composed of those elements which can be asserted in quantitative terms like resources, geography, economic growth and population etc. Intangible elements are non-quantitative like ideology, morale, leadership and diplomacy etc.

Broadly the elements of national power can be discussed under two main sub-categories i.e. Tangible elements and intangible elements.

**Tangible elements of national power:** Following are some of the tangible elements of National Power.

a. **Geographical location:** It plays an important part in the power of a nation. England used its peculiar geographical location to rule the whole world. Geographic location of Taiwan, Hong Kong and other regions of world have contributes much in its national power. Location of USA has helped her to save herself from disturbances and losses of all historical world wars.

b. **Natural Resources:** It contributes to the growth of national power. It includes minerals, oils, gas, coal, hydro-electric capacity etc. It is only due to the presence of oil fields majority of gulf countries are rich.
c. **Population:** It can be a positive point for growth or can be a burden on the economy of a nation. Educated population increases the national power. Moreover the population of a national should not be so small or too large.
d. **Industrial Capacity:** The economy of a country is known by its industrial power. China is increasing its national power because of its good production of industries. It was only due to Russian help in Indian industries that India started growing.
e. **Agricultural Capacity:** A country which produces surplus agriculture production is treated as more powerful than a country which has more agriculture imports. Before the Green Revolution in India, it also used to import more agriculture products (PL 480 with USA)
f. **Military Strength:** It is also one of the important elements of national power. It provides the security to its citizens and also increases its economy by Military Industrial Complex.
g. **Bureaucracy:** It also contributes a lot in the growth of a country. It helps the ministers in running government. They are supposed to be the technical, professional and permanent builders of a nation.

**Intangible Elements:** Following are some of the intangible elements of National Power.

a. **Type of Government:** A Democratic country is supposed to be more powerful than Socialist. Because democracy places the right and able candidate to right position. USA is today supposed to be more powerful than Russia due to this reason.

b. **Intelligence:** It provides very important input for the security of nation. Ranging from Kautilya to Machiavelli various thinkers have stressed to make this element strong. It is supposed to be the backbone beyond all security successes of a country.
c. **Quality of Diplomacy:** It is one of crucial element of national power. If a nation maintains a qualitative diplomacy it leads itself to the higher reaches of development. Diplomacy of Sh. Narinder Modi is its best example.
d. **National Morale:** It is the degree of determination with which a nation supports the foreign policies of its government in peace time as well as in war. National morale is never permanent and static. It changes with time and conditions particularly in democracy. It is a governmental oriented element.
e. **National Character:** It is citizen oriented element. It is the trait of people towards all the works of national life. It is outcome of evolutionary process and is attitude of previous generations which is transmitted to the next generations.
f. **Leadership:** It is one of the most important elements of national power. Right leadership takes right decision at right time which leads to making a nation powerful. Mao of China is one its best example.
g. **Foreign support and dependency:** Foreign support is also very important but a national should not totally dependent on foreign nations for all necessary items. Foreign support helped India to face USA aggression during 1971 war with Bangladesh.

**Conclusion:** It can be concluded from the above discussion that National power is determined by various elements. Ranging from population, natural resources, military strength, government to bureaucracy etc. all elements plays an active role in the development of a nation. A nation has no control for his few elements such as geographical location etc. but they perform better in Industry, military strength and intelligence etc. to make a nation powerful.

**National Interest: Meaning, nature and kinds**

National interests are those aims of the nation which it wants to achieve. In international politics it is very difficult to define the national interest because the interest of one state is mostly against the interest of other. Different thinkers have given different definitions regarding the national interest.

Frankel divides the various attempts to define national interest into two broad categories i.e. objective and subjective. The first are of the view that it can be defined with help of some objectivity while the second believe that it is a constantly changing pluralistic set of objective references. Just like every person has his life standard according to his financial and physical power same is the case with national interest of nation. Every nation tries to increase its power through its national interest. It is believed that democratic countries have a peaceful interest as compared to socialist countries because of expansionist nature of the latter. The realist thinkers propose a *realpolitik* view of national interest as offered by Machiavelli. They are of the view that the real interest of the nation is acquiring power in this anarchical world.

Frankel defined National Interest as '*amount to the sum total of all national values*'.

Hans J. Morgenthau defined National Interest in *terms of power*.

Vernon Van defined national interest is that '*which states seek to protect or achieve in relations to each other*'

**Types of national interest:**

Robinson divided it into 6 types

a. **Primary interest:** It is the basic interest of the country. It is also known as core or vital interest. These include preservation of Physical, political and cultural identity against possible encroachment from outside powers. E.g. particularly after 2014 India is building infrastructure near China border to secure its land near China borders. Moreover govt. organizes various programmes to promote Hindi against English in India.
b. **Secondary interest:** It includes protection of our citizens in other countries. Although less important than 1$^{st}$ but it is also

very important as it maintains a dignity of a nation at world level.

c. **Permanent interest:** It includes long term interests which are very important for the country. E.g. Determination of Britain to maintain freedom of navigation during past few centuries for protection of her overseas colonies and trade.
d. **Variable interest:** These include short term interest which changes with time. These relations are defined on power and decrease of power with time. After independence we had good relations with USSR but today we are more inclined towards USA.
e. **General interest:** Those interest which are beneficial for more than one nation. Various issues such as trade, economic and diplomat intercourse etc. are beneficial for all nations. It was general interest of Britain to maintain balance of power.
f. **Specific interest:** This interest disappears with passage of time. It was specific interest of Britain to independence of new countries for preserving balance of power.

In addition to six types he also gives three more i.e.

a. **Identical interest:** These are the common interest of the member states e.g. the interest of developing countries for New International Economic Order (NIEO) and reformation of UN etc.
b. **Complementary interest:** Through not identical interest but can become common on a particular issue such as Britain wanted the independence of Portugal against Spain because she wanted to control the Atlantic region.
c. **Conflicting interest:** These interests are against the countries and originate on some particular issue such as irrelevant speech against any country, voting against in the UN and Border disputes etc.

**Promotion of national interest:**

a. **Diplomacy:** It is one of the most important and oldest methods of promoting national interest. This method is used by all the countries of the world. Every country has its embassy or high commission in other countries. These help their citizens in other countries. They also celebrate various days in other countries such as Yoga day celebrated by Indian Embassy. It also helps to solve dispute between the countries.

b. **Alliance:** It is also important for an individual national but supposed to be dangerous for the stability and peace of the world. World war 1st and 2nd are the outcomes of the great alliances. Moreover the alliance of Russia with India particularly in war of 1971 with Pakistan has also benefited Indian much more. Protection of national security of Saudi Arabia by USA and Bhutan by India are also the outcomes of Alliance.

c. **Propaganda:** This method is used to pressurize the public of other country to reduce her morale. This method is used to make the bad image of the other nation in world politics. This method is used by China in general against all neighbouring countries particularly India. Pakistan also uses this method at various international institutions such as UN etc.

d. **Political warfareor Political Ideology**: This interest can be for making a state weak or can be to apply a new ideology in a country. Such as USA tries to enforce democracy in the newly independent countries. Same is the case with Russia which promotes its communist interest.

e. **Economic methods:** This method is used by a strong economic country against a financial weak country. China used this method by offering heavy loans for airports and Ports in other countries and then pressurizes them for transferring the control of that airport or port to China. This method was also used by USA by offering few dollars to Pakistan to purchase a military base for American soldiers during the war on terror with Afghanistan.

f. **Imperialism and colonialism:** This method was used by European countries in 18th and 19th century to boost their economy by using the resources of their colonial countries. Great Britain used this method to rule the world including USA and India.

g. **Coercive methods and war:** This method was used by the powerful country to boost their national interest against the weak countries. This method was used by the USA against the Middle East countries having oils fields. By this method the USA forces the Arabian countries to do their oil export business in US Dollars.

**Conclusion:** It can be concluded from the above discussion that national interest is very important for a country for her survival and growth. It can be a dynamic or static, peaceful or violent depending upon the ideology of the country. Every nation formulates its national interest depending upon its need of time and physical strength. Every national tries to increase its power through national interest directly or indirectly.

**Foreign Policy: Meaning nature and determinants**

A policy, which a state makes in relation toward another State, is called the foreign policy. Like industrial policy, educational policy, agriculture policy every state gives special attention to its foreign policy. Every country has different foreign policy towards different country. Moreover every country makes amendments in its foreign policy to a nation in response to the foreign policy of that country towards the former. Foreign policy is a dynamic concept as it changes with the need and time. Various thinkers have treated the foreign policy as the core of their writings such as Machiavelli and Kautilya. All the countries in the world have their foreign policy irrespective of their ideology weather it is democratic or communist country. The globalisation has made its significance more as none of the country could easily survive by alienating herself from rest of globalized world.

**Definitions:**

**Schleicher** defined it as "the actions of the govt. officials to influence human behaviour beyond the jurisdiction of their own state".

**Lincoln** defined it as "a key element in the process by which a state translates its broadly conceived goals and interests into concrete course of action to attain those objectives and preserve its interest".

**Schleicher** "The objectives, plans, and actions taken by a state relative to its external relationship"

**Rodee** "Foreign policy involves the formulation and implementation of a group of principles which shape the behaviour pattern of a state while negotiating with other states to protect or further its vital interest".

**Modelski** define foreign policy as "the system of activities evolved by communities for changing the behaviour of other states and for adjusting their own activities to the international environment".

Every state decides its own course of action in international relations in the light of its mean and ends. Then it conducts its foreign relations and behaves at international level and regulates the behaviour and actions of other states according to that action plan. This is called foreign policy.

**Determinants of Foreign Policy**: Various factors influence the making of the foreign policy of a country and these are called the determinants of the foreign policy. Even, majority of the determinants change with time and circumstances except basic need of the country. It is not possible to lay a general rule of determinants of foreign policy. Following are some of the determinants which are taken into account while making the foreign policy of a country.

a. **Geography:** It plays an important part while formulating foreign policy of a country. It becomes compulsory for a land locked country just as Nepal to have good relation with neighbours for her connectivity to the world. A country having surplus agriculture can export the material to the other country if having good relations with them.

b. **History and culture:** It also plays an important part in foreign policy formulation. It provides the basic guidelines for the foreign policy. Such as Indians are against the colonialism because we were under British. Culture also plays an important part just like we Indians are supposed to be peaceful nature because of our ancient peaceful culture.
c. **Economic Development:** It is also important for development of a nation. It forces a nation to have good relations with other countries to have good trade and attract the large Foreign Investment for development of a country. E.g. India has good relations with USA and Japan for economic development.
d. **National Interest:** It is also important factor for formation of foreign policy. A country achieves her national interest by her foreign policy. It establishes different foreign policy toward different country depending upon the need and situation.
e. **Political structure:** The political structure of a state and the nature of ruling elite also play a great role in the formulation of foreign policy. A democratic state is supposed to be have more peaceful foreign policy because of their accountability to public or parliament. Foreign policy changes with change in govt.
f. **Ideology:** Ideology is also a dominant factor in the formulation of foreign policy. The communist govt. is supposed to be of secret foreign policy but the democratic govt. is supposed to be of open foreign policy. Ideology can lead a country to the path of development or destruction.
g. **Public Opinion:** In a democracy it is impossible to ignore the opinion of public while formulating the foreign policy. E.g. in India various ministers resign due to some problems in the ministries such as Suresh Prabhu Union Minister of Railways submitted his resignation because of two major train accidents.
h. **Foreign Policy of other states:** Every state sets her foreign policy for every country in response of their foreign policy to that country. Such as recently India stopped import of palm oil from Indonesia in protest of their frequent attempts of highlighting at international level the fake intolerance against

Muslims in India.

i. **International Organizations:** Foreign policy is also affected by the international organisations. Various organizations such as UN have established rules for peaceful and open foreign policy. Various other organizations such as SAARC, ASEAN and BRICS help the member countries to solve their disputes and make a peaceful and favourable foreign policy towards each other.

CHAPTER THREE

# Instruments for Promotion of National Interests

**Diplomacy: Meaning, importance and types**

**Diplomacy:** The process of presentation and negotiation by which states customarily deal with the one another during the time of peace is called diplomacy. It is civilized process with which one state behaves with other state. It occupies an important position in the international relations. It is an instrument of foreign policy. It is a chariot to reach the destination set by states. It holds an important place in international relations for the survival of the State and peace in the world. Every national set their particular type of diplomacy to achieve national interest. Nature of diplomacy by a particular State also depends upon the ideological basis of the State. A democratic state is supposed to be having a peaceful diplomacy whereas a communist state is supposed to be having an aggressive and expansionist diplomacy.

**Definitions:** Different thinkers have defined it based on their own prospective. Some of the important definitions are given below;

Diplomacy in the popular sense means the employment of tact, shrewdness and skill in any negotiation and transaction. **Quincy Right**

Diplomacy is the management of international relations by negotiation **Oxford**

Diplomacy is the application of intelligence and tact to the conduct of official relations between the governments of independent states **Sir Earnest Satow**

Diplomacy thrives in Public view rather than in private international understanding. **Woodrow Wilson**

**Origin of Diplomacy:** Its origin can be traced to the times of the City States of ancient Greece. In 5th Century BC, there were frequent special missions between Greek City States. The Roman Empire also did a bit to improve this process of Greek diplomacy. They made an important contribution in the field of international law. They had skilled diplomats and trained observers. During middle age i.e. from the 6th century AD to late 14th century, diplomacy simple meant the study and the preservation of archives rather than the act of negotiation. Modern Diplomacy as a professional diplomacy arose in Italy in late middle age. The first known permanent mission was established in 1455 by the Duke of Milan. During the next century majority of the Italian City States were having permanent embassies in London, Paris and Court of Holy Roman Empire. For three hundred years this diplomacy was still diplomacy of Court. Its objective was to promote the interest of the foreigners abroad by various means. The character of diplomacy got a big boost with the Peace of Westphalia treaty. This treaty established the nation state system. Diplomats from all over the countries were represented in the court of Louis XIV. By the late 18th century the Industrial revolution in America and France changed the nature of diplomacy starting with new era of diplomacy.

The Congress of Vienna in 1819 made a lot of contribution to the nature of diplomacy. The congress laid down certain rules of procedures which are still commonly observed. The diplomatic hierarchy of four ranks was thus established.

a) Ambassadors

b) Papal Representatives

c) Envoys extra-ordinary and minister plenipotentiary

d) Minister resident and charge d'affairs.

Till the end of 18$^{th}$ century the diplomacy was branded as old or traditional diplomacy. The 19$^{th}$ century diplomacy better known as modern diplomacy demanded new methods, skilled and trained persons because of the change in nature of diplomacy

There were three methods on which traditional diplomacy was based i.e. Italian, French and German although the French method of diplomacy is usually known as traditional diplomacy. Traditional diplomacy was confined to Europe with five main powers i.e. England, France, Austria and Spain and even USA remained away until 1897. Old diplomacy believes that great powers have the special responsibility of maintaining world peace. Nicholson was of the view that while the old diplomacy was oligarchic, maleficent and obscure and new diplomacy is democratic, beneficent and limpid.

Chapter IV of UN deals with peaceful settlement of disputes i.e. from Art. 33 to Art 38. Art 33(1) The parties to any disputes which can disturb the peace of world shall seek a solution by negotiation, enquiry, mediation, conciliation, arbitration, judicial settlement, resort to regional agencies or arrangements or other peaceful means of their own choice.

Vienna Convention, 1961 defined a framework for diplomatic relations between independent countries. This convention was held on 4$^{th}$ of June and India ratified it on 15$^{th}$ October, 1965. This convention gives freedom to diplomats such as their bags are not opened or detained at the airport.

**Kinds of Diplomacy:** Broadly speaking there are two types of diplomacy one is closed diplomacy and other is open diplomacy. Closed diplomacy is also known as secret diplomacy or classical diplomacy and is used before the formation of League of Nation and also before the formation of UN. The credit of open diplomacy goes to Woodrow Wilson who pleaded for open diplomacy in his famous 14 points. In addition to these two types there are various types of diplomacy as mentioned below;

a. **Multilateral diplomacy/conference diplomacy:** It became popular after world war 1st. In this type of diplomacy representative of various country meet in the form of conference. It has been criticised by Harold Nicholson as 'perhaps the most unfortunate diplomatic method ever conceived'.
b. **Big Stick diplomacy:** It is a type of diplomacy used by USA and it was codified by the Theodore Roosevelt President of USA. This type of diplomacy involves threat of armed action for weak States and economic sanctions for powerful states.
c. **Personal/summit Diplomacy:** It involves direct participation of foreign ministers, head of states, Head of Govt. in diplomatic negotiation.
d. **Political Diplomacy:** This form of diplomacy focuses on solution of conflict by dialogue and negotiation.
e. **Military Diplomacy:** It focuses on military actions in achieving national interest and dealing with other nations. USA uses NATO as its military diplomacy on the basis of saving human right and democracy.
f. **Economic Diplomacy/Diplomacy of Development:** It is based on carrot and stick theory. It focuses on Trade and Aid.
g. **Nuclear Diplomacy:** It uses the power of a particular country mostly nuclear power in diplomatic negotiation. It is one of most dangerous as a single conflict can led this whole world to destruction.
h. **Cultural Diplomacy:** It mostly focuses on spreading own culture in other regions. Due to this type of diplomacy, British people have made English language as one of the most important language in the world.
a. **Oil Diplomacy:** It is one of the most important types of diplomacy. Middle East countries have used this diplomacy to control their relations with other countries of world. Due to this USA and India are having good relations with Israel as well as gulf countries particularly with Saudi Arabia. Moreover as the world is moving toward green fuel such as battery operated

vehicles so the middle east oil countries are going to lose their this dominance in the world.

j. **Coercive Diplomacy:** It is used by strong countries on the basis of their armed as well as nuclear power to achieve their national interest. Currently China is practicing it by extending her boundary disputes with neighbouring countries. USA also uses this for international trade of crude oil in dollar.

k. **Dollar Diplomacy:** USA also uses this for international trade of crude oil in dollar.With this diplomacy USA applies economic sanctions on various countries.

ax. **Vaccine Diplomacy:** It is one of the forms of medical diplomacy which became popular during COVID-19 pandemic period. In this process a country tries her best to improve the relation with other country by supplying COVID 19 vaccine to that country. India used this type of diplomacy during COVID 19 pandemic period.

all. **Shopkeeper Diplomacy:** It is characterized as practical open minded, compromising and candid. In this form of diplomacy a country behaves politely and tries her best to make good relation with other countries to boost her trade and finally economy.

n. **Wolf Warrior Diplomacy:** Used by China to criticise and threaten those countries which criticise Chinese aggressive policies. It is aggressive style of coercive diplomacy adopted by Chinese diplomats in the 21$^{st}$ century under Chinese leader Xi Jinping's administration. This term was coined from the Chinese action film 'Wolf Warrior'.

o. **Coalition Diplomacy**: Became famous after 2$^{nd}$ World War. In this anarchical world the coalition is a strategy to increase power of a country by making alliance with other country in order to survive.

UN under the Chairmanship of B. B Ghali UN published a report in 1995 known as '*An Agenda for Peace*'. This report gives sequence of the Process in Diplomacy i.e. Preventive Diplomacy, Peace Making, Peace Keeping and Peace Building.

**Importance of Diplomacy:** In this anarchical world it is very difficult for a nation to survive. Diplomacy is a process with which a country behaves in a civilized manner with other. Diplomacy is very important in international relations as it makes friendly relations with the other countries. Moreover with the help of diplomacy the small States survive by making their relation good with the powerful States. Grabbing of Bhutan territory by the Chinese is its good example. It was the diplomatic relations of India and Bhutan which forced India to send her defence forces to kick the Chinese soldiers from Doklam. It was the Indo-Russian good diplomatic relations which stopped American from interfering in 1971 India Pakistan War. History also shows that diplomacy established peace in Europe in $18^{th}$ and $19^{th}$ Century by balance of power. United Nations is also a gift of diplomacy which made it possible for the world to motive the States of the world for establishment of peace in this world. If every country will have good diplomatic relations with each other, there are more chances of peace in this world.

**Imperialism: Meaning, Nature and Instruments**

The word ***imperialism*** is very difficult to define. The communist countries have defined it with respect to the bad policies of the capitalist countries of the western democratic states. The democratic countries of the western world have explained and linked it with the expansionist nature of communist countries. The third world countries have defined it with respect to the colonialism of the western capitalist countries with which they have affected a lot. The word imperialism has been derived from the Latin word *'imperium'* meaning to Command or control. Imperialism is older concept dates back to the ancient empires and is most commonly related to Roman Empire.

Thus the term imperialism draws attention to the way one country exercise power over another, weather through settlement, sovereignty or indirect mechanism of control. It is the exercise of command or domination of one people by a stronger people. Therefore imperialism means pacification and domination.

**Definitions:** Following are the some of the important definitions of imperialism;

Imperialism is a policy which aims at creating, organising and maintaining an empire **Moritz Julius Bonn**

Imperialism means the domination of non-European native races by totally dissimilar European nations. **Parker T. Moon**

Imperialism is the expansion of state's power beyond its boundaries **Morgenthau**

Imperialism is purely economic term and it is the highest form of capitalism **Lenin**

Imperialism is the imposition by force and violence of alien rule upon subject people **Schumpter**

A look at the various definitions shows that different scholars have emphasised different aspects, however it is commonly held that it is a movement towards territorial expansion with implied economic interest. It is based on superior subordinate relationship. Besides territorial expansion it also believes in dominance in economic and cultural spheres.

Many powerful and ambitious nations tend to dominate and over others in order to boost their own domestic growth. This process is named as Imperialism and it has remained as a policy of pursuing and promoting national interest. Various countries particularly of European Continent have favoured it as their foreign policy. History shows that this tendency to dominate over others has been manifested in one or different periods. Changez Khan, Alexander, Nepolean, Bismark and Hitler etc. are its best examples.

Several methods were employed to successfully implement the policy of imperialism such as military intervention and wars, exploiting foreign markets, purchase of raw material and cheap labour etc. Moreover preaching some particular religion, culture and political system is also considered as a method of imperialism. In the developing countries the native people speaking English Language and wearing jeans are supposed to be superior and it is also a blessing of imperialism.

Factor contributing for growth of Imperialism:

1. **Industrial Revolution:** It leads to more production. In order to sell these more products the countries of Europe felt the need for markets and also the areas of raw materials. These developed countries searched various countries of Asia and Africa for getting workers for man power, raw material and selling the finally made products.
2. **Geographical Discoveries:** The discovery of new areas by the Travellers of Europe resulted in the formation of colonies. This process arranged majority of European states in competition with each other for colonies.
3. **Economic Considerations:** To boost their native economies, the countries of Europe searched for colonies to get market, raw material and cheap labour.
4. **Rehabilitation of surplus population:** Because of more population and less area various countries established their colonies and a fraction of population migrated to these new places. They were forced to work more for maintaining the production of factories.
5. **Cheap Labour:** To boost the industrial production the European countries were in need of cheap labour, so they established their colonies. They also migrated a lot of workers in industrial work from the agricultural sector. This migration was by force and not by will.
6. **Philosophical impact:** Various philosophers such as Kautilya, Machiavelli, Hegel, Nietzsche and Treitschke etc. contributed for the spread of imperialism. They believed that a country must acquire more land and resources in order to become more powerful. They are right on the scientific bases as increasing population needs more resources and grabbing area for the survival of increasing population was the most important and best method during that time. This process is expensive as it is fulfilled on the expenses of war and loss of humanity.
7. **Aggressive Nationalism:** Hitler in Germany and Mussolini in Italy used this technique to mobilize a lot of people on name of nationalism. They favoured the policy of imperialism to acquire

more land and become the rule of a single world government.

8. **Improvement in means of communication:** The policy of imperialism became possible only due to improvements in the means of transport and communication. To increase the trade and profit they established various means of communication. Introduction of Railways in India by British people was its best example.
9. **Religion:** Various Christen missionaries made themselves busy in preaching their religion. This process also contributed for imperialism. In India a large section of society got converted into Christianity. Tribal people were converted more as they were the backward and unaware section of the Indian society.

### Neo-Imperialism: Meaning Nature and Instruments

With the development in the means of communication and awareness among the developing countries, the imperialism has changed its shape and the new face of imperialism is known by the name of neo-imperialism. Imperialism have under-developed the third world countries. When the imperial powers became weak after the Second World War they thought it difficult to manage the vast colonial area and hence switched to neo-imperialism. Moreover after the independence of third world countries, they become aware about the negative impacts of imperialism and started opposing it. As these newly independent countries were not so much aware about the system of governance, and they were facing various problems ranging from poverty and hunger to economic security. Keeping in view the need of these developing countries the imperial powers started to dominate the economy as well as the political system of these developing countries indirectly and it is known by the name of neo-imperialism.

It is process in which powerful countries offer financial aid, technology etc. to the developing countries so as to control the country and with this exploiting the resources of that country for personal use. Threat as well as military use is its important indicator. Just as Great Britain was among the top countries in case of imperialism in the same sense USA is holding its top position in case of neo-imperialism by its financial aid, economic sanctions as well as military actions.

Some people believe that imperialism as well as neo-imperialism has their merits as well as demerits. Some people believe that it is beneficial for both the master countries as well as colonial countries. The master countries preached the concept of constitution, law, human rights and democracy in the colonial countries. Other sections of people hold that master countries instead of developing these countries they made them still poor by making the exploitation of their resources.

**Factors promoting neo-imperialism:** Following are some of the factors which promoted the neo-imperialism in this world.

a. **Awareness against imperialism:** During the movement against the colonial rule for independence of the country people become aware about the imperialism of the western countries. When they became aware about imperialism the western countries modified their strategy and gave birth to neo-imperialism.
b. **Loss with War:** With the two world wars the powerful countries suffered the loss. The Second World War made the condition of these countries very bad. These countries were not able to control their vast colonial empire so they switched to neo-imperialism to recover the loss of war through the colonial countries.
c. **Change in structure of power:** Every war results in the movement of power from one party to another. Same was the case with the two world wars especially with Second World War. After Second World War the structure of power shifted from United Kingdom to the United States of America. USA opposed the colonial system as she was also once having the colony of United Kingdom. Before war period United Kingdom was the countries having vast colonial empire. As she become weak after the war, she gave freedom to the various colonial

countries including India and switched to neo-imperialism.

d. **Political Freedom:** After the independence of various colonial countries, these countries become politically independent. It was not possible for imperial powers to control their territory directly. So by giving the offer of development they made the newly independent countries fool by diluting their culture, economy and foreign policy on the name of so called development.
e. **Communism:** Communist system criticised the capitalist system which was the main ideology beyond the imperialism. They mostly criticised the industrialization and privatisation for making the very bad condition of working class. So imperialism itself modified to neo-imperialism to make survival of this ideology in new era.
f. **Cold War:** During the cold war there was grouping of countries between the allies of United States and USSR. During this period they preached their ideologies as a result of which various regions of the world are even disturbed even today. With the increase in the power of colonial nations by joining the military groups of USA and USSR it was possible to capture a nation as was possible in imperialism so the powerful countries led to new invention known as neo-imperialism.
g. **Nuclear Weapons:** Nuclear age changed the power structure of countries in the anarchical world. After the nuclear weapons the world changed. This also led to the preaching of neo-imperialism for the security of native nations.
h. **Military Industrial Complex:** It is also one of important factor for the beginning of neo-imperialism. This is the only reason that India and Russia are the best friends for ever in this anarchical world. The need for survival in this anarchical world to the developing country and motive of profit and boosting economy to powerful countries promoted the neo-imperialism.
a. **Globalization:** It appreciates the neo-imperialism by connecting the world. Today's world believes in liberalisation, privatization and Globalisation. This process has led to spread the western

culture including English speaking and wearing jeans in non-western countries.

j. **Bretton Woods Institutions:** They also promote the biased economic system and hence the neo-imperialism. Third world countries have opposed this system and are demanding the New International Economic Order (NIEO) to reduce thedominance of western democracies.

k. **World Trade Organisation:** It favours free trade which results in the decline of the native industries. This organisation is biased as it favours the developed countries and is not suitable for under developed or developing countries. This process leads to increase in the catchment area of neo-imperialism.

## Region and Regionalism with special refrence to ASEAN, EU and SCO

As the term denotes, regionalism is associated with region. Let us first of all define region. In the geographical sense, it means any more or less extensive part of the earth's surface. In political science it has a distinct meaning. It means a part of world marked by homogeneity in respect of language, cultural and community of economic and other interest etc. This term is used in different ways. On the one hand regions are the territories within the state, occasionally crossing the borders. On the other hand regions are particularly the areas of the world, comprising a number of different sovereign states.

***Cambridge dictionary*** defines the region as 'a particular area or part of the world or any of the large official area which a country is divided'.

The regionalism is a territorial concept but in real sense it is also a psychological concept like nationalism which provides we-feeling among the regional groupings. Regionalism is a basic as well as local term. It can be seen everywhere ranging from a *Mohalla*, Village, State and Nation to the world level. It is an integrative force to the one region and divisive force to the other region. While fostering loyalty toward a region it opposes the intra nation and world level organisation such as UNO.

The ***Encyclopaedia of Social Sciences*** defines regionalism as "a counter movement to any exaggerated or aggressive form of centralization. It must not however, be considered solely from political point of view or government administration. Regional problems arise only when there is combination of two or more such factors as geographical isolation, independent historical traditionalism, radical, ethnic or religious peculiarities and local and economic class interests".

***Palmer*** and ***Perkins*** defined religion as "invariably an area embracing the territories of three or more states. Regionalism is a process of integrating on regional basis for some specific issues such as trade, social development or even security".

***Cambridge Dictionary*** defines regionalism as "a feeling of loyalty to a particular part of a country and a wish for it to be more political independent".

In the last several decades regionalism has become one of the forces challenging the traditional centrality of the states in International affairs. Russett, Cantori, Spiegel, Falk, Mendlovitz, Nye, Myrdal, Lindberg and Scheingold are some of the chief exponents of regional approach. These states are bound together by ties of common interest as well as geography. Regionalism includes three theories as discussed below;

a. **Functionalism:** This theory is also known as liberal institutionalism. This theory applied the concept of national interest as the uniting elements of various nations. For the realization of their interest many nations take the help of institutions. It arose as a philosophy which visualized a gradual evolution of a peaceful, unified and cooperative world. Its main thinker is David Mitrany and his celebrated work is "***A Working Peace System***". In his work he explained the functionalism. According to him when two or more countries co-operate in some functions such as the technical and economic fields of interdependence they will benefit and eventually result in habits of co-operation and deeper understanding of each other. With this benefit and mutual understanding they will also co-operate in other functions. This effect is known as *spillover* effect. This process will lead to foundation of peaceful working of the state system. This process is called functionalism. He is also known as father of functionalism. Other thinkers related to this theory are Leonard Woolf, Norman Angel, Robert Cecil and G.D.H Cole. The functionalism does not aim at creating world federation structure rather they seek to build '*peace by piece*' through transnational organizations that emphasis the '*sharing of sovereignty instead of its total surrender*'. They are of the view that none of the government will surrender its sovereignty therefore they suggest a peaceful slow process. They lay emphasis on socio-economic and welfare needs than the political needs. They believe that men go to work not for political but socio-economic needs. They treat economic, technical, scientific, social and cultural fields as functional sectors. Mitrany thinks of '*one solid international block of flats*' instead of '*detached national houses*'. David Mitrany was of the view that co-operation among technical experts in a functional area will result in the creation of international agency what will push the national state to co-operate rather than wage war. Karl Popper have criticised this concept by saying that 'piecemeal social engineering not for the architects or purveyors of blueprints'.

b. **Neo-Functionalism:** This theory is an improvement upon functionalism and redefines the same by analysing the impact of functionalism on national states. This approach focuses on the integration process in Europe. It proposes a regional integration as against to global integration suggested by functionalist. In order to solve their disputes, national states might mingle together to such an extent that they put their own sovereignty at stake. They may step further toward a federal structure of peaceful coexistence, mutual understanding and cooperation in socio-economic sphere. It arose as a critique of functionalism along with the most celebrated works of Ernest B. Hass. Leon

N. Lindberg, J P Sewell, Laurence Scheinman, Karl Kaiser and Scheingold are some other exponents of neo-functionalism. Some of the important works related to it are; *Beyond the national state: Functionalism and international organization* written by Ernest B. Hass, *The uniting of Europe: Political, Social and Economic Forces, 1950 – 1957* written by Ernest B. Hass, *Political Community and the North American Area* written by Karl Deutsch and *France Germany and The Western Alliance: A Study of Elite Attitude on European Integration and World Politics* written by Karl Deutsch.

c. **Inter-governmentalism:** It is a reaction to neo-functionalism. It was put forward by ***Putnam***. According to this theory, the sovereignty and the national interest of a state do not vanish because of regional integration, rather it maximises the power of the states for more regional, intergovernmental accords, bargains, trade agreement and so on.

## ASEAN

Association of South East Asian Nations was created on 8th August 1967 through Bangkok Declaration by Indonesia, Malaysia, Philippines, Singapore and Thailand. The leaders of these countries felt its need because of Vietnam War with USA and various other political problems. Brunei joined it in 1984, Vietnam in 1995, Laos and Myanmar in 997 and Cambodia in 1999. Currently its total members are 10. These countries are shown below in map.

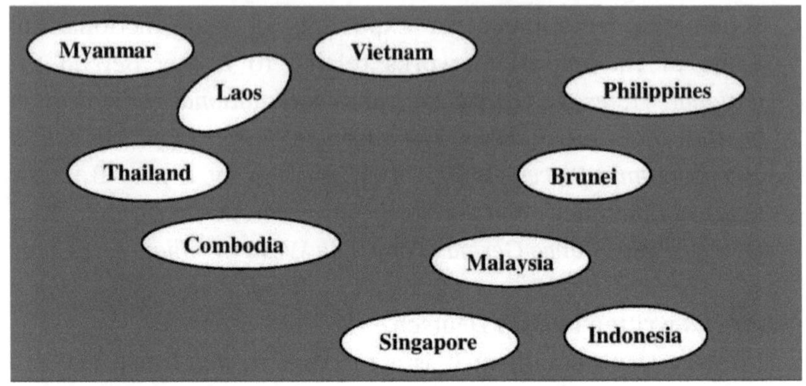


**Rough Map Showing ASEAN Member countries**

**Dialogue Partners**

a. Australia
b. Canada
c. European Union
d. Japan
e. New Zealand
f. United States
g. China (Became on 1996)
h. India (1996)
a. Republic of Korea (1991)
j. Russia (1996)
k. United Nations Development Programme (1997)

Pakistan is sectoral dialogue partner (dialogue partner in few sectors such as environment and education etc.)

**Some of its aims are**

a. To accelerate the economic growth, social progress and cultural development in the region
b. To promote regional peace and stability

c. To promote active collaboration and mutual assistance on matter of common interest.
d. To provide assistance to each other in the matter of training and research
e. To promote South East Asian studies
f. To collaborate for greater utilisation of their agriculture and industry
g. To maintain close and beneficial cooperation with existing international and regional organisations.

**Body of ASEAN**

a. Ministerial Conference
b. Standing Committee
c. Secretariat.
d. Permanent Committees
e. Ad-hoc Committees

Secretary General of ASEAN was appointed on merit for five years.

**ASEAN plus three:** It includes China, Japan and South Korea.

East Asian Summit (EAS) was formed in 2005 and it includes 18 countries. It has formed with inspiration from ASEAN plus three. It includes Australia, China, India, Japan, New Zealand, Republic of Korea, Russian Federation and USA. Zone of Peace, Freedom and Neutrality (ZOPFAN) was declared it in 1971. SEAN members have signed The Treaty of Amity and Cooperation in South Asia (TAC) in 1976.

**India's Relation with ASEAN:** Narasimha Rao Government in India announced its Look East Policy in 1991 with a priority to build relations with ASEAN. The major interest was to build economic relations. India became Sectoral Dialogue Partner in 1992 and full dialogue partner in 1995. It finally concluded the Free Trade Area in Goods and Services with ASEAN in 2014. India also forged to Bay of Bengal Initiative for Multi-Sectoral Technical and Economic Co-operation (BIMSTEC) and Mekong Ganga Co-operation as sub regional grouping to connect with ASEAN. India started the Act East policy in 2014 with an aim to focus more on ASEAN. As the Look East Policy mainly focused on economic co-operation, Act East Policy included security, terrorism, urban renewal, piracy and climate change etc. India has also participated in ASEAN Defence Ministers Meeting. The Act East Policy has announced that Connectivity, Culture and Commerce i.e. 3Cs shall be the priority of India. In Act East Policy Modi ji highlighted that the vision of India for the region is SAGAR i.e. Security for all and Growth for All.

**ASEAN Regional Forum (ARF):** It was Formed in 1994 and focuses on three factors i.e. Promotion of confidence building, development of preventive diplomacy and elaboration of approaches to conflict. It includes 10 members including dialogue partners, North Korea, South Korea and Mongolia. India became its member in 1996.

**Treaty on South East Asia Nuclear Weapons Free Zone (SEANWFZ):** All the ten members signed this treaty on 15th December 1997. First Indian ASEAN summit was held in 2008.

**European Union**

Among all the regional organisations it is the most successful one in terms of trade and development in the region. It was foundedon 1st Nov. 1993 at Maastricht in Netherland. Currently 27 states are its members. It represents 5.8% of world population including 71 % Christen & 45 Catholics. Its GDP is 17.1 trillion which is about the 18 % of World GDP. 1n 2012 EU was awarded Nobel Prize. Its slogan is '***United in Diversity***'. It has 24 official languages including, three main languages i.e. English, French and German. Following are the important points about it

**Members of EU**

Austria, Belgium, Bulgaria, Croatia, Cyprus, Czech Republic, Demark, Estonia, Finland, France, Germany, Greece, Hungary, Ireland, Italy, Latvia, Lithuania, Luxembourg, Malta, Netherlands, Poland, Portugal, Romania, Slovakia, Slovenia, Spain and Sweden.

These countries are also shown in map above.

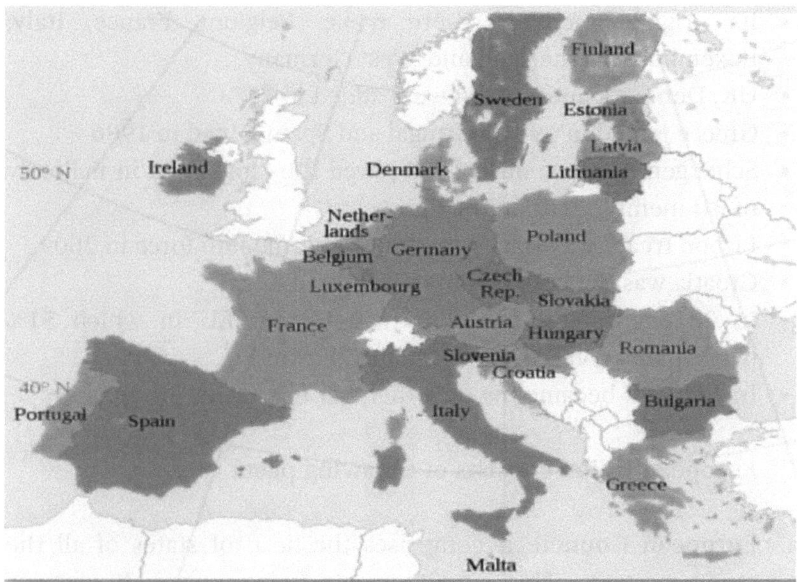


**Image showing European Union Member Countries**

**EU common Currency:**

**Following 8 countries have established their common currency**

Bulgaria, Czech Republic, Denmark, Croatia, Hungary, Poland, Romania and Sweden

**History of Formation of EU**

- European Coal and Steel Community (ECSC) formed in 1951 by Treaty of Paris
- European Economic Community (EEC) formed in 1957 by Treaty of Rome
- European Atomic Energy Community (Euratom) was established in 1958 by above treaty.

- ECC was renamed as European Community by Maastricht treaty in 1993.
- Its original members were 6 i.e. Belgium, France, Italy, Luxemburg, Netherland and West Germany.
- UK, Denmark and Ireland were added in 1973.
- Greece joined in 1981, Portugal and Spain joined in 1986
- Schengen Agreement in 1985 paved the movement in majority of EU member without passport.
- Lisbon treaty was signed in 2007 and came into force in 2009.
- Croatia was the last state to be admitted in EU.
- In 2016 a referendum was held to exit EU in which 51% participants voted for its withdrawal from EU.
- In 2020 UK became the only member to left this group.

**European Union consists of following parts**

a. **European Council:** It comprises the head of states of all the member states. This council meets twice a year. It elects a president who holds the office for six months. The council take all decisions on the basis of unanimity.
b. **Council of Ministers:** It consists of the Foreign Ministers of the member states. These members represent the interest of their countries rather than the interest of EU. This council meets at least once a month and take all decisions.
c. **European Parliament:** It is a large body consisting representatives of all the member states. These are elected by the legislatives of the respective states.
d. **European Commission:** It consists of 20 members appointed for a term of five years. It takes all decisions on the basis of majority votes.
e. **European Court of Justice:** Its members are appointed for a term of 6 years.

**Important Treaties in European Union:**

a. **Treaty of Paris:** This treaty was signed in 1951 by France, Italy, West Germany, Belgium, Luxemburg and Netherland establishing the European Coal and Steel Community. This treaty came into force in 1952 and expired in 2002.
b. **Treaty of Rome:** This treaty was signed in 1957 by Belgium, France, Italy, Luxemburg, Netherland and West Germany. It came into effect in 1958. It to formation European Atomic Energy Community and is also known as Euratom Treaty. This treaty led to the creation of European Economic Community best known as the European Community.
c. **Merger Treaty:** This treaty was signed in 1965 and came into force in in 1967. This treaty was signed in Brussels and is also known as treaty of Brussels. It merged three institutions i.e. European Coal and Steel Community, European Atomic Energy Community and the European Economic Community.
d. **Single European Act:** It was signed in 1986. It was first major revision of 1957 Treaty of Rome.It set a target of setting single EU market by 1992.
e. **Maastricht Treaty:** It was signed in 1992 and came into effect in 1993. It laid the foundation of European Union.
f. **Treaty of Amsterdam:** It was signed in 1997 and was made effective from 1999. It also amended the treaties which made the European Community. Under this treaty member states agreed to transfer certain powers from national governments to European Parliament.
g. **Treaty of Nice:** It was signed in 2000 and came into effect in 2003. It amended the treaty of Rome and Treaty of Maastricht. Its main aim was to reform the institutional structure of EU to face the contemporary challenges.
h. **Treaty of Lisbon:** Signed in 2007 and came to force in 2009. It amended two important treaties which form constitutional basis of EU.

**Indian & European Union:**

i. India is EU's 10th largest trading partner with 2.1 % of EU's overall trade whereas EU is India's third largest trading partner after USA and China. First Indo-EU Summit was held in 2000 at Lisbon.

## War: Meaning, Types and Changing Nature

**War:** Conflict and war had been a regular feature of the human history. Since the beginning of human being they restored to war for common good. Majority of the philosophers believe that to avoid these wars and get security, human being established the institution of state by a social contract. Different thinkers have given different definitions of war depending their way of thinking about its causes. Some of the definitions are given below;

War is the use of organized force between two human groups pursuing contradictory policies each group seeking to impose its policy upon the others **Hoffman Nickerson**

A contention between two or more states through their armed forces, for the purpose of overpowering each other and imposing such condition of peace as the victory pleases **Prof Oppenheim**

The legal condition which equally permits two or more hostile groups to carry on a conflict by armed forces **Quincy Wright**

War is to national life what winds are to the sea **Hegel**

As war is one of the most destructive method of achieving power but still it has favoured by various thinkers. Hegel holds that war is a useful instrument because it saves the nations from stagnation, inertia and backwardness and greatly contributes to its progress. Various thinkers have some new concepts in war such as ***New War*** by Mary Kaldor, ***Degenerated War*** by Martin Shaw and ***Hyperbolic War*** by Raymond Aron etc.

**Changing Nature of Warfare:** Approaches to understanding warfare in the immediate years after the Second World War had a residual impact of the experiences of the two Great Wars. These wars were total world wars. ***Karl Von Clausewitz*** (1780-1831) was an untypical Prussian military officer because he was a scholar in uniform. He proved to be a philosopher in his own right. Modern scholars have placed him on the same pedestal as Karl Marx, Adam Smith etc. Clausewitz fought against Napoleonic France and then distilled his experience in writing. His philosophical treatise titled *Vom Kriege* (***On War***) was published in 1832 by his widow ***Maria Von Clausewitz***.

Clausewitz's analysis of warfare turned out to be one of the best ever produced in history. For Clausewitz, war is organized violence unleashed by the state. He divided war into Limited War and Real or Absolute War. For him, eighteenth century European warfare as practised by Louis XIV and Frederick the Great represented Limited War. In contrast, Napoleon Bonaparte, whom he admiringly called the ***'God of War'***, tried to break out of the paradigm of Limited Warfare. For Clausewitz, Napoleonic Warfare exhibited seeds of Absolute War that would reach fruition in near future. Clausewitz's prophecy proved true but he did not live to witness Absolute Wars of 1914-18 and 1939-45. So, what we mean by Modern War is Clausewitz's early forms of Real or Absolute War. Thus, Modern War is the stage between Limited War of the eighteenth century.

The French Revolution ushered in the idea of destruction of the enemy's government. Hence, the beginning of French Revolution i.e. 1789 could be taken as the beginning of Modern War. This process reached its logical culmination under Adolf Hitler's Total War when the objective was complete destruction of enemy's society by wholesale mobilization of the common people.

The concept of limited war as it originally developed focussed on the conflicts between the two superpowers that were fought, not on their soil or directly fought in other areas of the world. Therefore, when one tries to understand the 'limited' nature of limited war, the focus is on of the abundant military power that both the superpowers have but do not actually use in such a war.

Strategic Defence Initiative (SDI) was a research programme that was to investigate the feasibility of new defensive technologies based in space. The new technologies aimed to detect, track and destroy the Soviet missiles. The detection would be done from the point of its takeoff; the tracking would continue throughout its flight path and the destruction of the attacking missile would be done any time from its take off until its last stage of zeroing onto the target. Some works on are given below;

War is the father of all things Heraklitos

God is on the side of heavier battalions Napoleon Bonaparte

Defence of the West Liddell Hart

Introduction to Strategy Andre Beaufre

**Conclusion:** It can be concluded that since the beginning this humanity on earth the nature and influence of war have changes. Initially the war was limited to a group of persons with their swords but as the humanity developed with time, this concept of war was also changed. The first change appeared with the rulers of state kept professional and trained persons in their army. This reached to its topmost position with the manufacturing of Atomic and Hydrogen bombs. Today in the age of nuclear weapons it has the capacity for the destruction of humanity in this world. Moreover the curiosity of human being towards is still increasing even after nuclear weapons, the biological weapons and now a day the use artificial intelligence in the defence sector this artificial development is still going on.

CHAPTER FOUR

# Management of Power

## Cold War: Meaning, Phases and Détente

The two major conflict of 2nd half of the twentieth century are the discord between the East and West and between the rich countries of North and Poor countries of South. The former is known as Cold War and the latter is known as *North South Divide.* Sometimes the western democratic countries are also called *Free World* and the communist countries as *Red Communist.*

**Meaning of Cold War:** Bernard Baruch, an American Statesman in an address in Columbia South Carolina on April 16, 1947 a month after ***Truman Doctrine*** said that "*let us not be deceived – today we are in the midst of the Cold War*". Cold War is also known as '***Hot War or Propaganda War***'.

**Origin of Cold War:** The word '***Cold War***' was coined by ***Bernard Baruch,*** a US Statesman. It was further popularized by Walter Lippmann, a print media person of USA.

**Causes of Cold War:** There are mainly three branches of thinkers tracing the causes of Cold War i.e. Orthodox, Revisionist and Objective. Orthodox hold that USSR was responsible for Cold War, Revisionist hold that USA was responsible for it, where as those holding objective view holds that both USA & USSR were responsible for it. Following are some of the causes of Cold War;

a. **Second front:** First cause of Cold War was opening of second front against German Forces. USSR demanded for it in 1941 but USA opened it in 1944.

b. **Germany and Poland:** They both differ on German and Polish govt.
c. **Lend Lease aid:** USA suspended Lend Lease aid to USSR.
d. **Potsdam Conference:** In this conference USSR demanded goods & worth 20 billion dollars should be ceased from Germany and its 50 % should be given to USSR and remaining 50% to USA & Britain.
e. **Article 'X' or 'Long Telegram'**: George F Kenning the than US Ambassador to USSR send a long telegram to USA. He said 'in these circumstances it is clear that the main element of any US policy toward the Soviet Union must be that of a long term, patient but firm and vigilant containment of Russian expansive tendencies'. This article was published and is known as ***article 'X'***. It is also known as ***'Long Telegram'***.
f. **Truman Doctrine:** Truman declared on 12 March 1947 that 'I believe that it must be the policy of the US to support the free peoples who are resisting attempted subjugation by armed minorities or by outside pressure'. It is known as Truman Doctrine and it comes under *The Policy of Containment* which aimed to stop soviet expansion an influence. It was especially for Turkey and Greece.
g. **Marshal Doctrine/Marshal Plan:** 5 June 1947, it was for Western European states and it was the extension of Truman Doctrine.
h. **Molotov Plan:** It was a plan of USSR in July 1947 in response to US Marshal plan. It was a series of bilateral agreements linking USSR with East European Countries. This was an economic response to Marshal Plan. The political response was given in Communist Information Bureau (COMINFORM) in Sept. 1947 to provide Moscow with the institutional means to control foreign communist parties.
a. **Brussels Pact:** It was done in March 1948 by European states. It was a mutual defence treaty, which directed the signatory to extend military support to any member in case of an attack by Germany or any third party in Europe.

j. **Forces in Iran:** USSR refused to withdraw forces from Iran.
k. **Berlin Blockade:** In 1948 Berlin was blocked by USSR for 324 days. This resulted in formation of NATO in 1949.
ax. **USSR entry into nuclear club:** USSR became a nuclear power in 1949.
all. **Uniting for Peace Resolution**: It was passed in 1950 in the matter of Korean War.
n. **Germany after W. W. 2nd**: After the W W 2 Germany was occupied and governed by Allied Control Council.
o. **Korean War:** North Korea supported arms by USSR and army by China where South Korea supported by USA on basis of United Nation.
p. **ANZUS:** Australia, New Zealand and USA defence grouping formed on 1st Sept. 1951.
q. **Japan Peace Treaty:** It was held on Sept. 8 1951.

**Causes between 1953 – 1962**

a. Policy of Peaceful co-existence of capitalism and socialism by Khrushchev.
b. In 1953 US did an agreement with South Korea to provide security to it.
c. South East Asian Treaty Organization (SEATO) was signed in 24 February 1955. It is also known as Manila Pack. It has eight members including USA, UK, France, Pakistan, Australia, New Zealand, Thailand and Philippines.
d. Extension of Truman Doctrine to entire Middle East by the name of Eisenhower Doctrine of 1954.
e. Middle East Defence Organization was signed in 1954.
f. Baghdad pack was signed in 1954 by U.K., Turkey, Pakistan, Iran and Iraq.
g. CENTO was formed in 1955 by Iraq, Iran, Turkey, Pakistan and England.
h. Vietnam Crisis 1955.

a. WARSAW group formed by USSR with 12 East European communist states on May 14, 1955. It was a response to NATO of USA. It has a total 8 countries i.e. Albania, Bulgaria, Hungary, Poland, West Germany, Romania and Czechoslovakia.
j. Federal Republic of Germany on 5 May, 1955 supported by USA & German Democratic Republic supported by USSR.
k. American exploded Thermonuclear or hydrogen bomb in 1952 and USSR nine months later.
l. During Suez Crisis of 1956 USA refused to take side of her allied i.e. Britain and France. When USSR sided with Egypt, USA gave help to Britain and France in the shape of Eisenhower Doctrine in January 1957. Its aim was the contamination of communism at international level. It was having same aim as of Truman Doctrine for Greece and Turkey.
m. Khrushchev visited USA in 1959.
n. U-2 Aircraft incident.
o. 25 Mile Long Berlin Wall was constructed to check the fleeing of refuges from East to West Berlin.
p. Cuban Missile Crisis 1962 forced the two powers to come close for easing the tension which ultimately paved the way for Détente.

**Thaw in the Cold War 1963 -1968**

a. Geneva Summit
b. Camp David meeting 1959 is related to Berlin (German) problem.
c. Hotline 1963 between White House & Kremlin.
d. Partial Test Ban Treaty (PTBT) 1963.
e. Outer Space Treaty 1967.
f. Nuclear Non-proliferation Treaty 1968.

**Détente, 1969-1978:**

It was easing of strained relations between USA and USSR during Cold War. President Nixon and his national security advisor

Henry A Kissinger were responsible for it. Kissinger defined it as 'an environment in which competitors can regulate and restraint their differences and ultimately move from competition to cooperation'. Détente was the official name of US policy toward USSR. Some of important conferences related to it are;

a. Strategic Arms Limitation Treaty (SALT) 1972.
b. 35 Nation European Security conference in Helsinki 1973.
c. 35 Nation European Security conference in Belgrade 1977.

**End of Détente:**

Czechoslovakia experienced ***Prague Spring*** or ***Socialism with human face***, under ***Alexander Dubehek*** in 1967 who decided to withdraw from the WARSAW Pack. Soon Brezhnev proclaimed that is known as ***Brezhnev Doctrine*** which stipulates in no uncertain terms that a communist state was within its rights when it intervenes in the internal affairs of an East European state if such action would prevent the re-introduction of a capitalist social system. Some incidents related to it are;

a. Brezhnev Doctrine 1967
b. Indo-Pak war of 1971
c. Liberation of Bangladesh
d. Six day war between Israel and Arab brotherhood.
e. Yom Kippur war between Israel Vs Egypt & Syria.

**New Cold War**

a. **Soviet invasion of Afghanistan:** USSR invaded the Afghanistan and USA supported the Afghanistan.
b. **Carter Doctrine:** It declared American's willingness to use military force to protect its interest in the Persian Gulf. Any attempt by any outside force to gain control will be regarded as assault on the vital interest of USA.

c. **New cold war**: It began during the tenure of Ronald Reagan and Brezhnev. Brezhnev said 'Russia declares détente with the USA as dead'.
d. **Reagan Doctrine:** He pledged US support to anti-communists insurgents to overthrow Soviet supported governments in Afghanistan, Angola and Nicaragua.
e. **Star War:** President Reagan took the war to space and started his Strategic Defence Initiative (SDI) dubbed as Star War. It was a research programme to explore opportunities of space based defence against ballistic missiles.

New Détente started with the announcement of democratic reforms in USSR known as Glasnost (openness) and Perestroika (political and economic restricting).

**End of Cold War:** Following are the summits which contributed for end of the cold war.

a. Geneva Summit 1985
b. Reykjavik Summit 1986
c. Washington Summit 1987
d. INF Treaty
e. Moscow Summit 1988
f. Malta Summit 1989, between Bush and Gorbachev.
g. Moscow Summit 1991
h. In Feb 1992 Bush and Yeltsin made a formal declaration regarding the end of Cold War.
a. At London Summit NATO leaders announced formal end of Cold War.

**Balance of Power: Meaning, Devices and its contemporary relevance**

Balance of power as the name indicates is a philosophy or an ideology which believes that a single powerful must be balanced by the other so that there can be established the peace in the world. This concept believes that if there will be single powerful country in the world it can declare war on any other but if there will be another country (or group of country) with comparatively more or less power, there are less chances of such a war. This is an old concept of maintaining peace in the world. The traditional relations among independent states are often explained in terms of balance of power.

Contemporary writers have called this theory as '*a basic principle of international relations*'. Idealist have long condemned balance of power because in their view it is related to power politics. On the other hand realists have defended it on the ground that moral rules cannot be applied in international affairs and that the pursuit of balance of power leads to the *greatest goods of the greatest number*. Winston Churchill, Kenneth Thompson and Hans J. Morgenthau treat it as a foreign policy. Martin Wright, A J P Taylor and Charles Lerche see balance of power as a system. Woodrow Wilson disregards for balance of power stems from the tendency to treat balance of power as a symbol of the realist philosophy. Louise Halle, John Morton Blum and Reinhold Neibuhr have all maintained that Wilson denied the reality of power in IR. Dina Zinnes have discussed seven and Martin Wight has discussed nine meaning of balance of power.

***Herbert Butterfield*** refers balance of power as 'mechanistically self-adjusting and self-rectifying'. ***Inis Claude*** treat it as 'semi-automatics'. The balance of power of 18$^{th}$ century rested on the existence of five or six major powers.

***John Herz*** and ***Ernst Haas*** would choose the 18$^{th}$ century whereas ***Gulielmo Ferro*** and ***Henry Kissinger*** would choose 19$^{th}$ century as the period of greatest success of balance of power. But the period from end of Napoleon war to the 1$^{st}$ world war i.e. 1815 to 1914 are supposed to the golden days of balance of power. During the Napoleon era England and France were two powerful countries. After Napoleon defeat England, Prussia, Russia and Austria together balanced France. After the end of 19$^{th}$ century France and Russia was together balanced by Germany, Italy and Austria. Some of the scholars hold that the concept of balance of power is relevant today as well as in future and these are ***Louis Halle, Arnold Wolfers*** and ***Dewitt Poole. Waltz*** is of the view that if other countries were allowed to acquire nuclear weapons, the present bipolar system would be transformed into multipolar system. Along with him, ***Karl Deutsch, David Singer*** and ***John Stoessinger*** also hold the same view. Today's world is bi-multipolarity, which means two bigger power USA and USSR with other multipolar countries. ***Louis Halle, John Morton Blum*** and ***Reinhold Niebuhr*** have all treated balance of power as realist philosophy. ***Morgenthau*** have used it in four different ways i.e. as a policy aimed at a certain state of affairs, as an actual state of affairs, as an approximately equal distribution of power and as any distribution of power. ***Schleicher*** has discussed three, Haas as eight, ***Zinnes*** seven and ***Wight*** nine meanings of balance of power.

Some thinkers have regarded period between Treaty of Westphalia in 1648 French Revolution of 1789 is regarded as 1$^{st}$ ***golden age*** of balance of power. Treaty of Utrecht 1713 is also an example of balance of power in Europe. The Congress of Vienna 1815 also established new balance of power. Triple Entente was found in 1907 by France, England and Russia and Triple Alliance in 1882 by Germany, Austria-Hungary and Italy. Morgenthau has criticized balance of power on three counts i.e. on its Uncertainty, Its unreality and its inadequacy.

**Methods of attaining balance of power:** Following are some of the methods for attaining balance of power.

a. **Alliance and Counter Alliance**: Alliances are formed to make a strong power group. In order to counter the alliance the opponent countries make another alliance to balance the first alliance.
b. **Compensation:** Annexation of division of territory e.g. Treaty of Utrecht divided the Spanish procession in Europe and outside among the Hapsburg and Bourbons. Participation of Germany under treaty of Versailles.

c. **Buffer State:** A state which comes between two states is called buffer state. Nepal is a buffer state between India and China.
d. **Armament and Disarmament:** Treaty of Versailles 1919, Washington Naval Treaty 1922, Partial Test Ban Treaty 1963, Strategic Arms Limited Treaty (SALT 1) 1972, SALT 11 1979, Intermediate Range Nuclear Force (INF) 1987, Strategic Arms Reduction Treaty (START) 1991. Some other done under UN are Non Proliferation Treaty (NPT) and Comprehensive Test Ban Treaty (CTBT)
e. **Intervention and non-intervention:** A third country may intervene between two or more states to balance the power. USSR made her intervention in 1971 Indo-Pak war to balance the power of USA by Supporting India against Pakistan and USA.
f. **Divide and Rule:** It is one of the oldest policies and also used by British govt. to make India a weak state.

***Richard Cobden*** was of the view that "the balance of power is a chimera". Others were of the view that there is no balance of power and there is 'balance of terror'.

# Old Papers

**Old Paper (University of Jammu)**

BA VI Semester Examination CBCS

Political Science Course No: USPSTC - 602

*Time Allowed* 2.5 hr *Maximum Marks: 80*

Note: The question paper consists of three sections.

**Section A:** Includes five compulsory short answer type questions. Each question in this section is of 3 marks to be answered in 70 - 80 words. (5X3 = 15)

**Section B:** Consists of five compulsory medium answer type questions. Each question in this section is of 7 marks to be answered in 250 – 300 words. (5X7 =35)

**Section C:** This section consists of 4 long answer type questions. The candidates have to attempt 2 out of these 4 questions with upper limit of 300 - 400 words. Each question carries 15 marks. (2X15 = 30)

**Section A**

1. Discuss the evolution of International Politics?
2. Explain the origin of European Union?
3. What was the Brasilia Declaration?
4. What do you meant by Nuclear Proliferation?
5. What are the main provisions of Stockholm Convention of 1972?

**Section B**

1. 'International Politics is a struggle for power and peace' discuss?
2. Discuss the Diplomacy as an instrument of foreign Policy?
3. Explain the structure and function of International Monetary Fund (IMF)?
4. Explain the relationship between State security and Human Security?

5. Discuss the efforts of United Nations in the mainstream of International Peace and Security?

## Section C

11. Explain the major stages of evolution of International Politics?
12. Explain the Origin, structure and functioning of World Trade Organization (WTO).
13. Make a critical analysis of Politics of Global war on terror?
14. Write an essay on the Gender perspective on International Politics?

Printed by Libri Plureos GmbH in Hamburg,
Germany